W9-BLE-892

ENVIRONMENT

Explorations in Environmental Science

Science Action Labs

Written by Edward Shevick

Illustrated by Leo Abbett

Teaching & Learning Company

1204 Buchanan St., P.O. Box 10
Carthage, IL 62321-0010

FRANKLIN PIERCE
COLLEGE LIBRARY
RINDGE, N.

This book belongs to

_____

The activity portrayed on the front cover is described on pages 36-37.

Cover design by Kelly Bollin

Copyright © 1998, Teaching & Learning Company

ISBN No. 1-57310-137-0

Printing No. 987654321

Teaching & Learning Company
1204 Buchanan St., P.O. Box 10
Carthage, IL 62321-0010

The purchase of this book entitles teachers to make copies for use in their individual classrooms only. This book, or any part of it, may not be reproduced in any form for any other purposes without prior written permission from the Teaching & Learning Company. It is strictly prohibited to reproduce any part of this book for an entire school or school district, or for commercial resale.

All rights reserved. Printed in the United States of America.

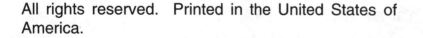

Table of Contents
Science Action Labs

Dear Teacher or Parent,

The spirit of Sir Isaac Newton will be with you and your students in this book. Newton loved science, math and experimenting. He explained the laws of gravity. He demonstrated the nature of light. He discovered how planets stay in orbit around our sun.

These labs are the product of many years of classroom science teaching. They have been used and revised based upon the hands-on experience of a wide variety of students. Pick and choose those that fit your personal approach to science teaching. Add, delete or modify to fit your style and your students' needs. Nothing I have written is engraved in stone. Place your personal imprint on them. Enjoy them as you enrich your students' lab activities.

The labs in this booklet are designed to be used directly with students and to help them understand the science involved in our many environmental problems. The background material and instructions are written for the students. The assumption is that they are organized and graded as lab teams. Simply copy what you need for each class. Note that **Materials Needed** and **For the Teacher** are at the end of each lab. Delete those parts when copying for student use.

Every teacher guide is supposed to have a basic philosophy. Mine is expressed in the goals listed below. They are based upon many years of meeting students' hands-on science needs.

The environmental approach used in this book is rational rather than hysterical. The author recognizes the severity of the environmental problems. Yet, he has faith that people will do the right thing for our Earth. He also has faith that science can overcome many of the problems.

It is sad that so many people are underfed. Still, advances in corn and rice growing technology make it possible to feed everyone. Recycling programs have been extremely successful. More fuel-efficient transportation is being developed as well as new energy sources.

Goals of a Laboratory Lesson

- To involve students in their science education.
- To get the teacher out of the dominant role and into the role of pot stirrer.
- To provide opportunities for creative process oriented thinking.
- To enable students to hypothesize and test their hypotheses within the limits of their background and laboratory materials.
- To provide opportunities for handling science apparatus.
- To let students enjoy sciencing.
- To provide opportunities for interaction of ideas within a group.
- To open new horizons in science education for the students.
- To confront students with some of the "unsolvable" aspects of science.
- To encourage the synthesis of their background facts and concepts in application to new problems.
- To provide "barriers" to make students conscious of their own limitations and thus encourage independent or classroom pursuit of science studies.
- To develop an appreciation for the fact that science can progress through a series of failures.
- To encourage careful observation and measurement.
- To accentuate the partnership of math and science.
- To encourage the big idea—the large conceptual pattern rather than the minute and isolated fact.
- To provide opportunities to summarize findings and to try to bring order out of apparent chaos.
- To encourage students to apply the same thought processes to other areas of their lives.

Sincerely,

Ed

Edward Shevick

TLC10137 Copyright © Teaching & Learning Company, Carthage, IL 62321-0010

Philosophy for a Successful Science Program

In our education as science teachers, we have been repeatedly exposed to long lists of steps in the scientific method. In educating our own science students, we have also stressed the scientific method. Somehow, in all those process lists, we have forgotten that the scientist himself or herself is central to the scientific method. His or her intelligence, curiosity, scholastic skills, rational skills, humor and personality all play a part in creative science.

The central person in any science program is the youngster who could become a scientist or at least scientifically literate. Studies show that most beginning high school students have lost their motivation and ability to question and be curious. Contributing to this motivation loss are teachers and curricula that fail to recognize the characteristics and needs of these youngsters who have so much to offer society. The nature and beauty of science education is that it is capable of rekindling the intellectuality and curiosity of youngsters. Following are some elements in a successful science program:

Variety. Provide a variety of outlets for their intellectual curiosity. Plan for a variety of learning experiences both within the day and the semester. Minimize rote drills.

Time. Allow students sufficient time to generate ideas and incubate concepts. Full development of ideas may require periods of independent or isolated thinking.

Skills. Develop skills in reading, typing, library use, computer use and process science.

Interaction. Ample opportunity should be given for interaction between students, teachers and supportive adults. They should develop a sensitivity to others and an acceptance of non-conformity.

Evaluation. Let the students share in assessing their strengths and weaknesses. Don't assign arbitrary and old-fashioned standards to youngsters.

Creativity. Encourage creativity by being creative yourself. Be willing to "risk" a new kind of experience. You'll soon find your creativity mirrored in your students' activity as they try new approaches without fear of failure.

Independence. Children need a maximum of freedom and autonomy. Provide opportunities for self-directed discoveries and divergent thinking.

Acceptance. Try to accept their ideas even though they appear to be unorthodox. Accept their positions and feelings. Prepare them to accept some failure in their experiments.

Honesty. Demand the highest level of intellectual and personal honesty in their experiments and reports. Always expect their best work.

Maturity. Students are still children with fears, egos and problems. They may need your help in adjusting to your classroom environment.

TLC10137 Copyright © Teaching & Learning Company, Carthage, IL 62321-0010

How to Have a Successful Lab
For the Student

Creativity. You are encouraged to be original and ingenious in carrying out the laboratory assignments. Do new things or find new ways to do old things. Be creative in gathering materials for the laboratory, in handling the materials and especially in making reports to your teacher or your class.

Initiative. You will be expected to do as much as you possibly can on your own. Study your text for background knowledge and then use the concepts you have studied to solve the problem at hand. If you definitely need help, ask your teacher, but do not expect him or her to give you all the answers. He or she will merely spin you in the right direction and leave the rest to you.

Concepts. As you do the laboratory investigations, use the major concepts you have studied in the text and in class to solve the specific problems you find. Concepts are the big ideas of science.

Math and Accuracy. Many of the investigations involve measurement, data gathering, organizing and graphing. You will find that these methods often provide information that cannot be obtained in any other way. To be a competent science student, therefore, you need to be an accurate mathematician.

Reports. Write your laboratory reports in such a way that they are neat, accurate and complete. Fill in all data, question and conclusion sections.

Materials. Simple materials are called for in many investigations. Help the class progress by bringing in as much as you can.

Safety. Think safety. If you have the slightest doubt about safe procedure, check with your teacher. Do not endanger yourself, your classmates or your equipment.

Cleanup. You and your teammates will be expected to keep your laboratory area clean and cooperate with your teacher in cleaning up the room when the laboratory period is over.

Teams. In most of the laboratories you will be working with teams of four. By doing this, you can help one another with the investigations just as professional scientists cooperate with one another to coordinate their activities.

TLC10137 Copyright © Teaching & Learning Company, Carthage, IL 62321-0010

Trapping Smog Particles

What Is Smog?

Smog is a form of air pollution. It is a combination of the words *smoke* and *fog*. Smog can be a result of weather conditions such as lack of wind or cool air holding down warm air. Mountain ranges near cities help trap and increase smog.

Our homes, factories, power plants and automobiles all cause smog. Sunlight acting on some smog ingredients creates even more harmful smog.

Smog contains invisible gases as well as solid particles. In this lab you are going to try and trap smog particles.

Preparing Your Smog Traps

1. Obtain four microscope slides and some petroleum jelly.

2. Use a toothpick or pencil to smooth the jelly over the *center only* of all four slides.

3. Cut four pieces of cardboard the *same* size as your glass slides.

4. Use a paper punch to punch a clean hole exactly in the center as shown.

5. Tape your cardboard cover to the glass slide. If done correctly, the smooth jelly should be just below the hole.

6. Place your slides in an envelope labeled with your name.

Now you have to decide on four places near your home or school where you will expose your slide to trap smog particles.

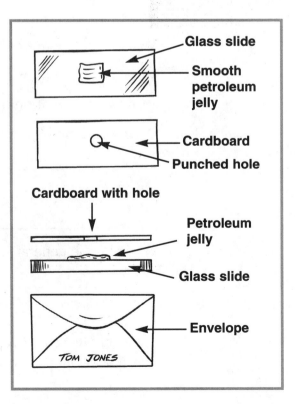

Glass slide

Smooth petroleum jelly

Cardboard

Punched hole

Cardboard with hole

Petroleum jelly

Glass slide

Envelope

TOM JONES

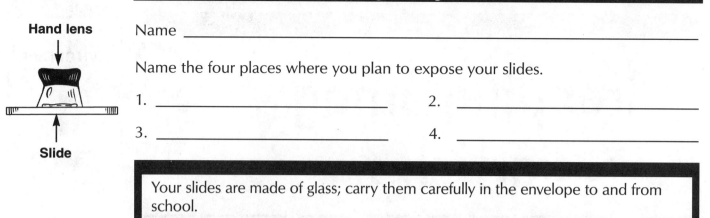

Hand lens

Slide

Name _____

Name the four places where you plan to expose your slides.

1. _____   2. _____

3. _____   4. _____

Your slides are made of glass; carry them carefully in the envelope to and from school.

7. Expose your slides for the three or four days and then return them to class for "Peering at Particles."

Peering at Particles

You will be observing your smog particles with either a hand lens or a microscope.

1. Observe your first slide. You will see many large and small particles. It is impossible to count them all. Ignore the very small ones and count only the reasonably sized particles.

What is the estimated particle count on the first slide? _____

Repeat using the other slides.

What is the count on the second slide? _____

What is the count on the third slide? _____

What is the count on the fourth slide? _____

Which slide had the most smog particles? Where was it exposed? _____

_____

Which slide had the least smog particles? Where was it exposed? _____

_____

Describe the general appearance of the smog particles that you collected.

_____

_____

Materials Needed: Microscope slides, petroleum jelly or cold cream, cardboard, hole punch, envelopes, toothpicks and hand lenses.

For the Teacher: Stress a smooth petroleum jelly surface.

TLC10137 Copyright © Teaching & Learning Company, Carthage, IL 62321-0010

Name _____

Investigating Smog

Our Unpure Air

Most American cities have done much to reduce air pollution levels. Air pollution is called **smog**. Smog can come from many sources, but the main polluters are factories, power plants, cars and trucks.

Smog can affect our lungs, throat, eyes, head and stomach. Smog can cause breathing problems, coughing, tearing, headaches and nausea.

Here are some of the harmful ingredients found in smog.

WHAT SMOG IS MADE OF		
Polluting Substance	**Source of Pollutant**	**Harmful Effect of Pollutant**
Sulfur Compounds	From burning coal and gasoline	Can kill plants and fish. Eats away at metal, stone, plastic and rubber.
Carbon Monoxide	Over 80% comes from auto exhausts	Can cause nausea, dizziness, drowsiness and, in extreme cases, death.
Carbon Dioxide	From burning coal, gasoline, gas and wood	Too much carbon dioxide can harm the Earth's atmosphere and possibly cause the Earth to warm.
Nitrogen Compounds	From power plants, autos, diesel engines and home furnaces	Forms nitric acid and results in acid rain.
Hydrocarbons	Auto and plane engines	Can cause lung cancer.

Describe any personal experiences you may have had on smoggy days. _____

_____

_____

TLC10137 Copyright © Teaching & Learning Company, Carthage, IL 62321-0010

Name _____

Dirty Windshields

You know that automobiles are a major source of smog. Can an automobile windshield help us learn about air pollution? Let's have a dirty windshield experiment. Have a few students volunteer to do the following and report back.

1. Wash your family car's windshield as clean as you can.

2. Leave the car out of the garage exposed to smog for 12 to 24 hours.

3. Use a clean white rag (such as a handkerchief) to wipe just half of the windshield.

   Describe the differences between the wiped and unwiped sides. _____

   _____

   _____

   Describe the white rag as best as you can. _____

   _____

   _____

> Your windshield and white rag only show the *solid* particles in smog. You cannot see any of the pollutants listed in the What Is Smog Made Of table. Most of them are invisible gases.

Dirty Auto Exhausts

What comes out of an auto exhaust pipe may surprise you. Here is an experiment **only a teacher or adult** should do to check exhaust gases.

> **Caution!** Only an adult should do this demonstration!

1. Obtain pliers and a long (at least 12" [30 cm]) strip of shiny metal.

TLC10137 Copyright © Teaching & Learning Company, Carthage, IL 62321-0010

Name _____

2. Let an auto engine idle for *one minute.*

3. Have the adult carefully use the pliers to place the shiny metal directly behind the exhaust.

4. Have the adult look away from the exhaust to avoid breathing fumes.

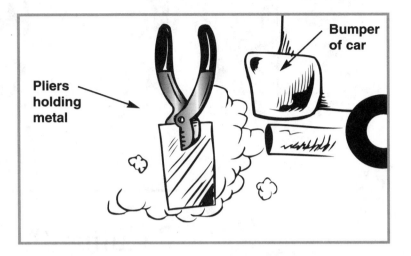

Pliers holding metal

Bumper of car

What do you observe on the piece of metal? _____

_____

_____

What might happen to the metal if left for hours near the exhaust? _____

_____

_____

_____

How might the windshield dirt and exhaust fumes affect your health? _____

_____

_____

Auto Pollution Research

There are many things being done to cut down on automobile air pollution. Research and report back on ways auto pollution is being reduced. Check with auto dealers and mechanics. Try the library or the internet. Call your local smog control agency.

TLC10137 Copyright © Teaching & Learning Company, Carthage, IL 62321-0010

Water Pollution Lab: How Sewage Kills Water Life

Polluting Our Water

Every year billions of tons of sewage and waste spill into our rivers, lakes and oceans. This water pollution comes from farms, factories and homes.

Without proper care, our water sources can become smelly, foul tasting and even deadly. Fish and plant life cannot thrive in polluted waters.

Why do fish suffer in sewage-filled waters? This lab will help you find out.

What is your hypothesis (educated guess) as to how sewage harms fish? _____

_____

_____

Sewage Substitution

We could mix sewage and fish, but this might be rough on the fish and your nose. Let's substitute a few things.

Sewage: Raisins will be used instead.

Decay Bacteria (which normally consume the sewage found in water): Yeast plants will be used instead.

Oxygen Detector: Methylene blue test solution will be used. Here's how it works.

When **oxygen** is present, it turns **blue**.

When **oxygen** is removed, it turns **light blue** or **clear**.

TLC10137 Copyright © Teaching & Learning Company, Carthage, IL 62321-0010

Name _____

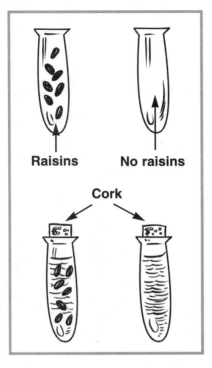

Raisins   **No raisins**

Cork

1. Place seven raisins (garbage) in one test tube. *The other test tube does not get any raisins.* It is your control.

2. Add $1/3$ teaspoon (1.6 ml) of yeast (decay bacteria) to *both* test tubes. Guess at $1/3$. The important thing is that both test tubes receive the *same* amount of yeast.

3. Fill *both* test tubes three-fourths full of oxygen detector solution. Both should be filled to the same height to insure a *controlled* experiment.

4. Place a cork into each test tube.

5. Place a thumb over each cork. Shake *both* test tubes very vigorously *three* times.

6. Place both test tubes back in the rack.

Answer the following questions while waiting for results:

What are the raisins substituting for? _____

What are the yeast plants substituting for? _____

What is the methylene blue supposed to measure changes in? _____

_____

_____

What should happen to the methylene blue solution if the decay bacteria (yeast) removes the oxygen? _____

_____

_____

What is the *only difference* between the test tubes (answer in terms of *sewage*)?

_____

_____

_____

Wait five to 10 minutes before going on to "Sewage Experiment Results."

Name _____

Sewage Experiment Results

Observe both test tubes carefully.

What difference do you observe between the raisin and nonraisin test tubes?

_____

_____

What must have been removed from the water by the decay bacteria (yeast) acting

on sewage (raisins)? _____

_____

_____

You must breathe to stay alive. What gas in the air around you is vital to your life?

_____

Fish must also breathe to stay alive. They use **gills** instead of lungs to breathe in

water. What gas must be dissolved in water for fish to survive? _____

_____

Sewage helps decay bacteria to grow. As decay bacteria grow, what gas do they

remove from lake water? _____

Sum up what you have learned about polluted water, bacteria and fish in two or

three sentences. _____

_____

_____

Materials Needed: Small corked test tubes, test tube holders, raisins, yeast and methylene
blue.

For the Teacher: Use a dark solution for methylene blue. Try to obtain yeast with little or
no added sugar.

TLC10137 Copyright © Teaching & Learning Company, Carthage, IL 62321-0010

Water, Water, Everywhere

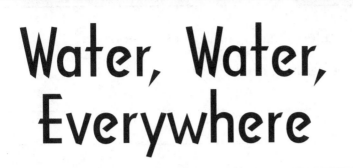

Our World of Water

Your body is 65% water. The Earth's surface is 70% water. Can you imagine a whale out of water? Could you boil an egg without water? Could you live without water? Could you cry or sweat without water?

The average person needs to take in about $2\frac{1}{2}$ quarts (2.4 l) of water every day. You also need water for cooking, bathing and lawn care. All totaled an average American consumes almost 100 gallons (378 l) of water per day.

Think about your personal use of water. Can you list 10 ways you use water?

1. _____ 2. _____

3. _____ 4. _____

5. _____ 6. _____

7. _____ 8. _____

9. _____ 10. _____

Eating Your Water

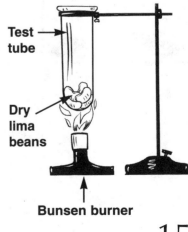

Test tube

Dry lima beans

Bunsen burner

Living things must take in water to survive. Animals, like yourself, drink some of the water they need. They obtain the rest of their water from the food they eat.

Many foods seem to be solid and dry, yet they contain much hidden water. Your teacher will demonstrate how seemingly dry foods have water inside.

TLC10137 Copyright © Teaching & Learning Company, Carthage, IL 62321-0010

Name _____

1. Your teacher will heat a few lima beans in a test tube or jar.

2. Describe what you see forming on the inside of the test tube. _____

_____

3. What do you think it is? _____

_____

4. Where must it have come from? _____

_____

Don't Expect Me to Grow Without Water

Lima beans and other seeds need more water than they contain in order to grow into plants. Let's experiment to find out how seeds take in water.

1. Line up five lima beans end to end as shown.

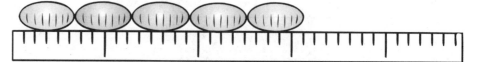

2. Measure the total length in millimeters. _____ millimeters

3. Place the five lima beans in a container of water. The water should be well above the beans.

4. Mark your container and store it overnight.

5. Line them up the next day and again measure the total length.

_____ millimeters

6. How many millimeters did they increase? _____ millimeters

7. Obtain a dry lima bean. Compare it with your soaked beans. Describe the differences. _____

_____

16

TLC10137 Copyright © Teaching & Learning Company, Carthage, IL 62321-0010

Name _____

Water Is Not Free

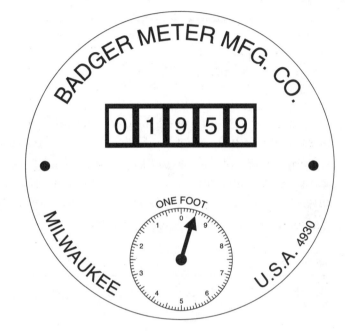

The water coming out of your faucet could come from a well, river or lake. The water must be purified and pumped to your home through a city-wide network of pipes.

Observe the water meter on the right. It measures your home use of water in cubic feet. It reads 1959 cubic feet. A cubic foot of water equals about 7 1/2 gallons (284 l). Some water meters read directly in gallons (liters).

Let's find out how much water you use in your home and at school.

1. Read your home water meter. _____ cubic feet or gallons

2. Read your home water meter about 24 hours later. _____ cubic feet or gallons

3. Subtract the first day's reading from the second day's reading. This gives you your daily water use. _____ cubic feet or gallons

4. Read your school water meter. _____ cubic feet or gallons

5. Read your school water meter about 24 hours later. _____ cubic feet or gallons

6. Subtract the readings to get your school's daily water use. _____ cubic feet or gallons

List some ways water could be saved at home and school. _____

_____

_____

_____

NEWTON'S
ACTION LAB

Environment
5

Water Goes Around and Around

Vital Water

Oceans cover 70% of the Earth's surface and contain 97% of the water available. Ocean water is salty. Only 3% of the Earth's water is fresh enough for human use.

Humans could not survive without water. Your body is two-thirds water by weight. Your blood is 92% water, and your brain is 75% water. Even dry appearing bones are 20% water. Your body uses water for digestion, circulation and temperature control.

Can you name some other ways that your body uses water? _____

_____

_____

Why do you think plants need water? _____

_____

The Water Cycle

Water moves from the oceans to the air and then back to Earth. This constant movement is called the *hydrologic* or *water cycle*. The sun is the source of energy for the hydrologic cycle.

Study the water cycle diagram. It shows how water travels from the Earth's surface to its atmosphere and then back again to the surface.

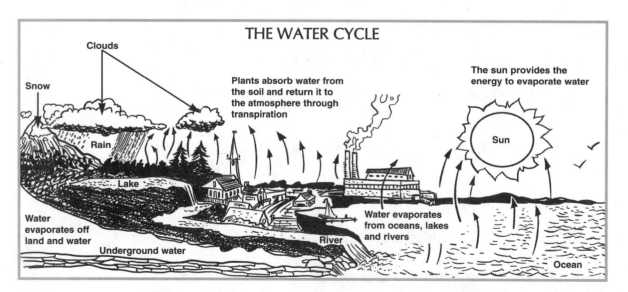

THE WATER CYCLE

Clouds

Snow

Plants absorb water from the soil and return it to the atmosphere through transpiration

The sun provides the energy to evaporate water

Sun

Rain

Lake

Water evaporates off land and water

Underground water

River

Water evaporates from oceans, lakes and rivers

Ocean

TLC10137 Copyright © Teaching & Learning Company, Carthage, IL 62321-0010

Name _____

What provides the energy to evaporate water from the Earth's surface?

Name some ways that water falls back to Earth. _____
_____

What two main forms of life take in and give off water? _____
_____

How does snow on a mountain get back to the ocean? _____
_____

Demonstrating the Water Cycle

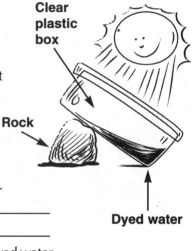

Clear plastic box

Rock

Dyed water

1. Obtain a clear plastic box with a lid. Plastic shoe boxes work fine.
2. Add a small paper cup of water to the box. Hot water makes the experiment work faster.
3. Add enough vegetable dye to give the water a dark color.
4. Place the clear lid on the plastic box.
5. Use a rock or "?" to prop the box up about 30° while it faces the sun.
6. Wait a few minutes until you see steam forming on the inside surface of the lid.

What provided the energy to evaporate the water? _____
_____

7. Observe the condensed water running down the top and side and back into the dyed water.

Is the evaporated water clear or dye colored? _____

In nature, salt, instead of dye, is in ocean water. What is left behind as the sun evaporates ocean water? _____

Water Fiction

The Earth is about 4.5 billion years old. The water cycle on the Earth today was probably around that long ago. It has been through the water cycle millions of times. The water has been in oceans, lakes, rivers, mountains and prairies. It has been part of dinosaurs and all kinds of plants.

It may have been part of Napoleon and Cleopatra. It may have been part of Presidents Washington and Lincoln. It may have cycled through scientists and singers.

Imagination time. Write a story which recycles a water molecule through one or more famous people of history. Use humor and exaggeration to provide an interesting mingling of your water molecule and your famous person.

TLC10137 Copyright © Teaching & Learning Company, Carthage, IL 62321-0010

Name _____

Acid Rain

How Acid Rain Pollutes

Acid rain affects the environment in many ways. It has been blamed for injuring forests and crops. It may also affect life in freshwater lakes and cause erosion of bridges and buildings.

The term *acid rain* covers more than just rain. It can fall to Earth as snow, fog or even solid particles.

Acid rain contains both sulfuric and nitric acids. Both are very harmful chemicals. Both acids are formed by sulfur and nitrogen products released by factories, power plants and cars. They are actually created in the atmosphere by pollutants mixing with cloud moisture. Laws are now in place to control auto and factory pollution. Scientists are studying how acid rain forms and are working on solutions to this environmental problem.

How Acid Rain Is Measured

Every material in the world is classified as being acid, base or neutral. Water is neutral. Vinegar is an acid. Soap is a base. Here is the scale used to test for acids and bases.

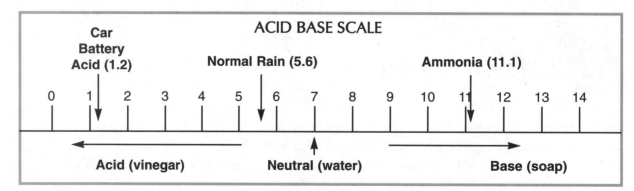

ACID BASE SCALE

Car Battery Acid (1.2)

Normal Rain (5.6)

Ammonia (11.1)

0 1 2 3 4 5 6 7 8 9 10 11 12 13 14

Acid (vinegar)   Neutral (water)   Base (soap)

Water is neutral and given the number 7. Acids are to the left. The lower the number, the more acidic a material is. The higher the number (up to 14), the more base a material is. Both strong acids and bases can be very dangerous to handle. They are to be avoided.

Rain is usually made of neutral water. Acid rain is a rain below 5.6 on the Acid Base Scale.

TLC10137 Copyright © Teaching & Learning Company, Carthage, IL 62321-0010

Name _____

Testing Acids and Bases

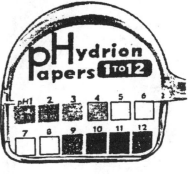

Acids and bases can be measured by a special kind of paper called pH paper. The paper changes color depending on the strength of the acid or base. You simply match the color with a chart to determine its acid or base number.

1. Obtain some pH paper.

2. Use it to test **liquid** materials.

3. List the materials and their number in the Acid Base Data Table on the right.

Here are some materials for you to bring in for testing. **Do not try to test any strong acids or bases.**

ammonia	milk	liquid soap
Milk of	soft drinks	baking soda
Magnesia™	saliva	solution
water	vinegar	rubbing alcohol
rainwater	apple juice	tomatoes
pool water	grapefruit juice	pickles
seawater	lemon juice	

ACID BASE DATA TABLE	
Materials Tested	**pH Number**
1.	
2.	
3.	
4.	
5.	
6.	
7.	

Solving the Acid Rain Problem

Many smart scientists are trying to solve our acid rain problems. You are now going to join them by coming up with some suggestions of your own. Don't be afraid to come up with some imaginative ideas. Write your ideas below.

_____

_____

_____

Name _____

Symbiosis Guessing Game

The Symbiosis Story

Everything in the environment affects everything else. Trees shade, feed and shelter living things. Ants go in and out of your home. Grass makes food for cattle and fresh oxygen to replace your exhaled carbon dioxide. Every plant and every animal have symbiotic relationships.

Symbiosis is an association of two unlike organisms. There are three kinds of symbiotic relationships listed below. Study them and any references available before you play the Symbiosis Guessing Game.

A.	**Mutualism:**	A symbiotic relationship that helps *both* organisms.
B.	**Commensalism:**	A symbiotic relationship where two organisms live together but *one* is helped. The other is not harmed.
C.	Parasitism:	A symbiotic relationship where the "guest" can be harmful to the "host" organism. A parasite can either kill its host or could be harmful but not fatal.

Symbiosis Guessing Game

Work with your team to fill in the blank spaces on the Symbiosis Guessing Game. You may use any references available. Make the best guesses you can. Your teacher will go over it later.

TLC10137 Copyright © Teaching & Learning Company, Carthage, IL 62321-0010

Name _____

SYMBIOSIS DATA TABLE (Fill in the blank spaces.)

Organism 1	Organism 2	Type of Symbiotic Relationship	Description of Relationships
Example: Shark	Sucker fish (Remora)	Commensalism	Sucker fish attach themselves to a shark and get a free ride, protection and scraps of food.
1. Cow	Man	Mutualism finally parasitism	
2. Mistletoe	Host plant		Host plant provides water and space in the sun. Mistletoe may kill host plant.
3. Legume Plant		Mutualism	Organism #2 provides nitrogen for plants. Legumes provide home for organism #2.
4. Green Plant	Animals	Mutualism	
5. Termite	One-celled animals that live in termite's stomach		Termite provides cellulose in form of wood for one-celled animals. One-celled animals break cellulose down into food the termite can digest.
6. Bee	Flowers	Mutualism	
7. Tapeworm	Human		Tapeworm lives in human intestines and absorbs food.
8. Ant	Aphids (sometimes called plant lice)		Ant provides protection to aphids. Aphids give off a form of food from their body for the ant.
9. Mother	Unborn child		
10.	Barnacle	Mostly commensalism but some parasitism	The barnacles attach themselves to this huge ocean mammal. Barnacles get free transportation. Host gets skin ulcer.
11. Algae	Fungi		Algae and fungi growing together form lichens. Algae provide the food and the fungi provide a moist base.
12. Wasp	Insect bodies		Wasp eggs grow in insect bodies and consume them for food as they develop.
13. Rhinoceros	Tick birds		Tick birds pick ticks (insects) off the rhinoceros and make noise to warn the rhinoceros of danger.

Materials Needed: You will need textbooks and various reference sources.

For the Teacher: This lab could be converted into a home research project for either teams or individual students.

Name _____

Soil Lab: Investigating the Earth

The Good Earth

Soil is a natural resource like coal, air and water. Scientists believe it takes nature 600 years to make 1" (2.5 cm) of rich soil. On and in this rich soil live many forms of plant and animal life. The limited amount of good soil available is vital to our survival.

Our environment begins with the soil beneath us. Conservation of the soil is essential if we are going to maintain high standards of living and provide for expanding populations. Our soils can become polluted by the careless addition of chemicals and by improper water drainage. They can be destroyed forever by wind and water erosion or by the intrusion of the sea.

Soil Profile

Water can be used to separate the different sized particles in soil. Place three teaspoons (15 ml) of soil in a tall test tube. Add water to the two-thirds level. Cork the tube and shake vigorously for one minute. Allow the tube to stand upright without shaking for five minutes.

1. In five minutes, your test tube of soil should have separated into layers.

2. Describe the differences between the top and bottom soil layers.

_____

_____

3. Save the test tube with soil for "How Sour Is Your Soil?"

Cork

Water 2/3 level

Soil

TLC10137 Copyright © Teaching & Learning Company, Carthage, IL 62321-0010

Name _____

How Sour Is Your Soil?

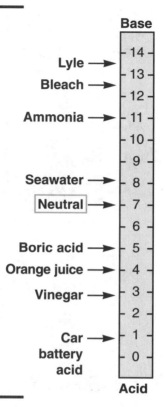

Vinegar tastes "sour" and is considered an *acid*. Soap tastes "bitter" and is considered a *base*. Soils can also be chemically acid or base. Some plants can't live in soil that is too acid or base. The chart on the right shows a pH scale used to measure acids and bases. You will be shown how to use pH paper.

1. Remove the cork from the test tube used previously.

2. Dip the end of your pH paper into the clear water at the top of your test tube.

3. What color did the pH paper turn? _____

4. What is its number on the pH scale? _____

5. Is your soil acid, base or neutral? _____

Base

Lyle → 14
Bleach → 13
         12
Ammonia → 11
         10
          9
Seawater → 8
Neutral → 7
          6
Boric acid → 5
Orange juice → 4
Vinegar → 3
          2
Car → 1
battery → 0
acid

Acid

There Is More Than Dirt in Soil

1. Place one teaspoon (5 ml) of rich soil in the bottom of a Petri dish. Spread it evenly along the bottom.

2. Cover with a Petri dish lid.

3. Place the covered dish in the sunlight or under a bright light.

4. Wait a few minutes.

5. What do you observe inside the Petri dish? _____

_____

6. Where must this moisture have come from? _____

_____

7. Why is it necessary for good soil to contain moisture? _____

_____

_____

Name _____

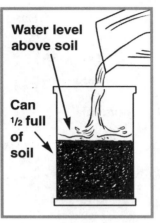

Water level above soil

Can ½ full of soil

8. Fill a small juice can half full of rich soil.

9. Add water slowly till you see something bubbling out of the water.

10. What do you observe bubbling out of the water? _____

_____

11. Where must it have come from? _____

12. Why is it necessary for good soil to contain air? _____

_____

How Fast Does Your Soil Drink?

Soils differ widely in their ability to absorb water. Sandy soils pass water through very quickly. It is difficult for water to penetrate clay soils. Let's find out how long your school soil takes to absorb water.

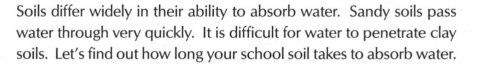

½ can of water

Open juice can

Soil

Can about 3 cm into soil

1. Your teacher will assign your team to an outside location.

2. Obtain a juice can that is open at both ends.

3. Press your juice can about three centimeters into the soil. **Caution! Watch out for rough edges**.

4. Pour one half of a juice can of water into the embedded can.

5. Time how long it takes for the water to penetrate. Stop when you see a muddy surface.

6. Record the time in seconds or minutes. _____

Soil Freedom

The standard soil experiments you have done only begin to scratch the surface in understanding soil. Your team is expected to carry on an independent investigation involving soil. A good start would be to study background information from texts, library books or encyclopedias. Decide on one investigation, and submit plans to your teacher for approval. You may use the following suggestions or ideas from your soil study.

TLC10137 Copyright © Teaching & Learning Company, Carthage, IL 62321-0010

Soil Lab: Investigating the Earth

Name _____

> **Hint:** Choose a soil problem that you are capable of handling with the resources and time available at the school. Don't expect the teacher to provide many special materials.

1. Your team should first spend some time researching soil.

2. Submit detailed plans of what your team proposes on _____.

3. Soil experiments will be carried out at school on _____.

4. A clear report on your soil lab and its results are due on _____.

Here are some suggested soil investigations. Feel free to research and develop your own ideas.

1. Compare two or three different kinds of soils using controlled experiments.

2. Soil density.

3. Soil moisture–heating and drying soil to determine its water content.

4. Erosion–testing on a small scale how soil erodes when water is poured on it.

5. Soil temperatures.

6. Capillarity–testing how long it takes and how much water can be pulled up into a jar of soil by capillary action.

7. Take a "bug" count of a small area of fertile soil.

8. Contrast sandy and clay soil for various characteristics.

9. Test for various chemicals in soil.

Research . . . Think . . . Plan

Materials Needed: You will need many juice cans. Cut both ends off some of the cans. You will need pH paper, large corked test tubes, Petri dishes and a supply of rich organic soil. Add some coarse sand or fine gravel to the soil in "Soil Profile."

For the Teacher: Take time to explain the use of pH paper. Perhaps show your class some sample color changes. The Petri dishes can be replaced by small baby food jars.

The "Soil Freedom" section is optional. Some students may want to work on soil at home. Require a valid scientific report that includes a detailed description of their plan, results, data collected and a summary of conclusions.

Name _____

Trees Are Not Just for the Birds

We Need Trees

Trees are our friends. They give us shade. They provide us with food. They shelter all kinds of insects and animals. They add beauty to our homes, highways and parks.

Trees carry on many important jobs that you might not be aware of. Water moves from the soil up through the tree roots and out through leaves to the atmosphere. This plays an important role in the water cycle that brings rain down upon the Earth.

You are an animal. You and all other animals take in oxygen from the air and convert it to carbon dioxide. If not for trees and other green plants, the Earth would run out of oxygen. Green, leafy trees absorb carbon dioxide and convert it back to oxygen.

Trees provide lumber for your house. Wood is converted to wood pulp to provide paper bags and cartons. The average American uses seven trees each year.

Here are some mixed up words. They all represent something we obtain from trees. Can you unscramble them?

1. YGOXEN __ __ __ __ __ __

2. DASHE __ __ __ __ __

3. BLUMRE __ __ __ __ __ __

4. NIURETRUF __ __ __ __ __ __ __ __ __

5. SOTAB __ __ __ __ __

6. NOMSLE __ __ __ __ __ __

7. BURBER __ __ __ __ __ __

TLC10137 Copyright © Teaching & Learning Company, Carthage, IL 62321-0010

Name _____

8. STUN ___ ___ ___ ___

9. LUFE ___ ___ ___ ___

10. RUPSY ___ ___ ___ ___ ___

Your teacher will help you with the answers. Can your team add six more things we obtain from trees?

1. _____   2. _____

3. _____   4. _____

5. _____   6. _____

How Tall Is Your Tree?

Trees are the largest of all plants. Most trees are about 20 feet (6 m) tall. A giant Sequoia can reach 250 feet (75 m) into the sky. You can measure how tall a tree is by measuring its shadow.

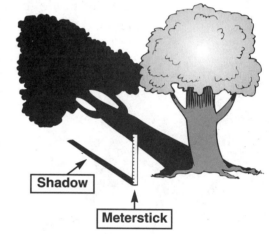

Shadow

Meterstick

1. Your teacher will assign your team to a particular tree.

2. Use a meterstick to measure the tree's shadow in centimeters. _____ centimeters

3. Place an upright meterstick in the sun.

4. Measure the stick's shadow in centimeters. _____ centimeters

Here's a math formula to work out the tree height.

$$\text{tree height} = \frac{\text{tree shadow} \times 100}{\text{stick shadow}}$$

Example: Assume a tree shadow of 400 centimeters. Let's assume a stick shadow of 50 centimeters:

$$\text{tree height} = \frac{400 \times 100}{50} = 800 \text{ centimeters}$$

5. Do the math for your tree and stick shadow. Round the answer off to the nearest whole centimeter. _____ centimeters

6. For your information, every 100 centimeters is equal to one meter or about three feet.

7. How tall is your tree in feet? _____ feet

Name _____

How Old Is Your Tree?

Trees continue to grow as long as they live. They get taller and wider.

You can find a tree's age and growth history exactly by drilling out a core from the bark to the center. It is also possible to **estimate** a tree's age by finding its diameter and dividing the diameter by the tree's average yearly growth. Since trees vary in growth from season to season, this is only a **guess**.

Let's estimate the age of four trees in your school environment. Your teacher has labeled them A, B, C and D.

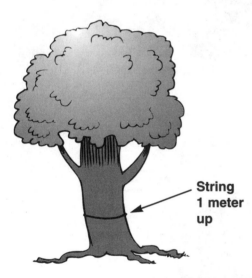

String 1 meter up

1. Assume an average growth rate of 0.6 centimeters per year.

2. Use a string to measure tree A's circumference one meter above the ground in centimeters.

3. Divide the circumference by 3.14 (π) to get the diameter in centimeters. Round off your answer to the nearest whole number of centimeters.

4. Divide the diameter by 0.6 to find the tree's age. Again, round off your answer to the nearest whole number.

5. Record your answers in the data table below.

6. Repeat for trees B, C and D.

ESTIMATED TREE AGE DATA TABLE

Tree	A	B	C	D
Estimated Age				

Bonus: The General Sherman Tree in California's Sequoia National Park is 1020 centimeters in diameter. Assume it grew 0.3 centimeters per year. How old would it be? Estimated age _____ years.

Materials Needed: You will need a meterstick and string.

For the Teacher: The rain forest plays a significant role in our environment. Perhaps you can have reports or a discussion on the rain forest's role.

Try to obtain some tree trunk cross sections. Counting rings give a tree's age. Dark rings represent summer growth. Light rings are spring growth. A thick ring means the tree had a good year in terms of water and weather.

TLC10137 Copyright © Teaching & Learning Company, Carthage, IL 62321-0010

Name _____

Acoustilab: A Challenge to Sound Pollution

An Attack on Our Eardrums

News Item: Airport Middle School forced to close due to excessive jet plane noise.

News Item: Studies at a university prove that young people who listen to loud music may suffer eventual hearing loss.

Noise is defined as "unwanted sound." The science of **acoustics** deals with the control of all sounds that reach our ears. Acoustical engineers work on soundproofing our homes, cars, factories and schools. They are concerned with controlling jet engine noises whose extreme sound energy can burst eardrums and cause convulsions.

Excessive sound can affect people in two ways. **Physiological** effects do something to our **bodies**. **Psychological** effects do something to our **minds**. Here is a list of ways that sound pollution can hurt people. They have all been taken from scientific studies.

1. Your team should read them over and discuss each one.

2. Draw a circle around the letter of each one that affects us physiologically.

3. Draw a triangle around the letter of each one that affects us psychologically.

a. Increases family tension

b. Destroys hair cells

c. Raises blood pressure

d. Causes headaches and nausea

e. Distracts people

f. Affects vision

g. Affects moods

h. Workers less efficient

i. Can trigger epileptic attacks

j. Decreases hearing ability

k. Causes ringing and hissing of ears

l. Increases irritability

m. Increases anxious feeling

n. Affects heartbeat

TLC10137 Copyright © Teaching & Learning Company, Carthage, IL 62321-0010

Name _____

How Noise Pollution Is Measured

Noise pollution is rated in units called **decibels**. Some standard sounds and their average decibel ratings are shown in the table on the left. Use them to estimate (guess) the typical sounds in the table on the right.

DECIBEL STANDARDS		DECIBEL ESTIMATES	
	Average Decibels		**Your Estimated Decibels**
1. Whisper	10-20	1. Teacher lecture	
2. Ordinary speech	60	2. Hall noises	
3. May damage human ear	85 and over	3. School bell	
4. Power lawn mower	110	4. Rock band	
5. Painful to ear	140	5. Fire engine	
6. Jet take-off	150	6. Freeway noises	
7. Can kill animals	165 and over	7. Teenager's radio	

Building an Acoustibox

In our attempt to create a quality environment in which people can be healthy and happy, we can't ignore increasing sound pollution. This lab will focus your attention on methods of absorbing sound energy. Your team will function as acoustical engineers to design materials that can quiet our lives. You will compete to design the world's greatest **acoustibox**.

HOW YOUR ACOUSTIBOX WILL LOOK

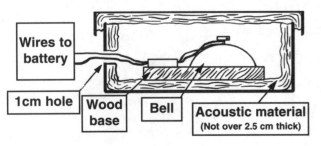

Wires to battery

1cm hole **Wood base** **Bell** **Acoustic material** (Not over 2.5 cm thick)

Acoustibox Requirements

1. It must be built inside a standard size cardboard shoe box. Your teacher will display a sample.

2. You may use any materials or combination of materials you wish to soundproof your box.

3. Special awards will be given for most clever use of materials. Don't be afraid to be different.

4. Fasten your materials to the sides, top and bottom of the shoe box with tape or glue.

5. At no point should the acoustic material be greater than 2.5 centimeters.

32

Name _____

6. Cut a one-centimeter hole through one side of the box as shown for bell wires to be shoved through. The hole should also pass through the acoustic material.

7. The shoe box lid and its acoustic material must still close completely over the box with the bell inside. Use rubber bands to hold the lid down.

8. Each team may enter two acoustiboxes.

9. You may use more than one kind of acoustic material in your acoustibox. No matter how many different materials you use, you can only have 2.5 centimeters of total thickness.

10. Your teacher will provide the bell and wires.

HOW YOUR ACOUSTIBOX WILL BE TESTED

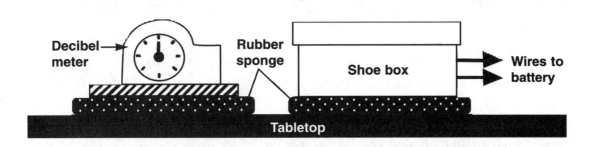

HOW YOUR TEAM WILL BE GRADED   POINTS

- For bringing in one acoustibox 4
- For bringing in a second acoustibox 2
- For clever use of materials . . . . .maximum 2
- For a full page, detailed colored drawing of the acoustibox .1
- For having the quietest acoustibox 2
- For having the 2nd, 3rd or 4th quietest acoustibox 1
- Total possible 12

This lab calls for a sound measuring device called a decibel meter. If not available, your teacher will assign one student to be Super-Ear. The Super-Ear will move slowly away from the acoustiboxes until no more sound is heard. Super-Ear will end up close to the best acoustibox and far away from the worst.

Materials Needed: You will need a standard shoe box as an example. You will need a loud bell or buzzer and a strong battery. It is better to use a bell transformer instead of a battery. Try to obtain a decibel meter if possible. You will also need a sponge rubber pad to place between the acoustiboxes and the table to lessen vibration.

For the Teacher: Get their attention at the start of this lab by secretly puncturing a balloon. This startles them into thinking about noise pollution. Give a bonus for any student bringing in a current article about noise pollution.

Use a trusted student as Super-Ear. Have Super-Ear remove his or her shoes and walk slowly away from the non-wire end of the acoustibox. Record distances to determine winners. It's all right to have multiple winners.

TLC10137 Copyright © Teaching & Learning Company, Carthage, IL 62321-0010

Name _____

Quackery Lab: Cheating the Consumer

What Is a Quack?

A quack is a person who cheats people by selling them "miracle" products. For hundreds of years, quacks have exploited fads, superstitions and fears to sell useless products. Many quacks claim to have instant cures for acne or cancer. Some promise longer life spans and instant hair growth for bald heads. They fool normally intelligent people into buying useless and even harmful food, drugs and consumer products.

Many false claims are even made for curing environmental problems. Some quacks peddle a super ingredient that will double your car's gas mileage. Some claim to cut air, water or sound pollution. Some are new energy sources that promise energy at little or no cost.

Joining the Quacks

In today's activity you are going to learn how quacks operate by "joining" them. Your team will develop a complete sales campaign for a **phony** health or environmental product. Use all your salesmanship for its promotion. Hopefully, you will see for yourselves that quacks can only be stopped by public agencies or by educated consumers.

1. Decide on one quack device or product to promote. The partial list in "Quackery Product Suggestions" can be used, or you can choose your own.

2. Construct a "gimmick." This can be a huge model pill, a fake electronic device, a food package or "?"

3. Design a full-page ad to be placed in a national magazine. Before you decide on your ad's layout, study magazine ads to determine how to have maximum emotional appeal. Feel free to use partial truths, references to false authorities, testimonials from cured people, hints about mysterious qualities or powers and money-back guarantees. Your ad must be on cardboard about 12" x 15" (30 x 38 cm) in size. Use color, cut-outs and a minimum of words to get your message across.

34

TLC10137 Copyright © Teaching & Learning Company, Carthage, IL 62321-0010

Name _____

4. Prepare a two-minute TV commercial to be presented to the class. Observe real TV commercials carefully to see how they get maximum "sell" into a short period of time. Display your "gimmick" during your TV commercial.

5. Your grade will be determined as follows: Maximum Points

   a. Imaginative quack product chosen 25

   b. Advertisement 25

   c. TV commercial–class presentation 25

   d. Gimmick–construction and originality 25

Quackery Product Suggestions

You may use an idea below or develop one of your own. Study how television and magazines sell their products.

1. A device that instantly purifies polluted water.

2. A mask to wear on smoggy days.

3. Edible garbage or packaging.

4. A pesticide that both kills insects and promotes plant growth.

5. An earplug that controls excess sound or blanks out TV commercials.

6. A powder that produces instant pure water without using any water.

7. Car engines that run forever, don't pollute and never need gasoline.

8. Clothing that will shield you from harmful radiation.

Here are some health consumer quackery suggestions:

liver pills	cancer salves
smoking cures	healing belts
exotic foods	reducing aids
miracle diet pills–for weight loss, gain or control	skin foods
	youth restorers
psycho quackery–cures for mental or emotional problems	blood purifiers
	baldness creams
nerve tonics	healing machines

For the Teacher: Allow time for planning and production of ads, gimmicks and TV commercials. Let humor prevail. This lab looks like a fun activity, but it ends up teaching students to be wary consumers.

TLC10137 Copyright © Teaching & Learning Company, Carthage, IL 62321-0010

Name _____

Survival: An Ecosystem Contest

Help! I'm Locked Up in an Ecosystem

Being alive is not easy. Living things have to take in food, water, minerals and air from their environment. If the environment is too hot or too cold or too wet or too dry, living things cannot survive. Living things cannot escape from their environment. Living plants and animals in their environment are called **ecosystems**.

Suppose you were locked up in a large sealed jar. The jar, the heat and the light would be your ecosystem.

1. What must be placed in the jar to keep you alive? _____

   _____

   _____

2. What might be placed in the jar that could continue to provide you

   with both food and oxygen? _____

   _____

   _____

Can You Keep Me Alive?

Here is another kind of ecosystem. The sealed jar contains a small fish, plants, gravel and a snail.

1. What does the fish give off that plants need? _____

   _____

   _____

TLC10137 Copyright © Teaching & Learning Company, Carthage, IL 62321-0010

Name _____

2. What part does the snail play in the ecosystem? **Hint:** What do animals like fish give off that could foul up the ecosystem? _____

_____

_____

Now for your ecosystem contest. Your teacher will provide the gallon jar, a standard size fish and a snail. Your teacher will not provide the water plants. What can your team place in the closed ecosystem to make your fish survive the longest?

a. Two teams may merge to make one ecosystem.

b. All special materials must be brought in by your team.

c. All ecosystems must be prepared and sealed in the classroom on _____.

d. Instructions for a standard ecosystem will be given in "Standard Ecosystem Requirements."

e. You are encouraged to vary your ecosystem to increase your fish's chances. See "Ecosystem Freedom."

f. Bonus points for the team whose ecosystem survives the longest.

g. Your fish will be observed each day. Fish that are having difficulty will be revived in the class aquarium.

h. Your captain's name and the date your ecosystem was sealed should be on a 3" x 5" (8 x 13 cm) card taped to the lid.

Standard Ecosystem Requirements

1. Feel free to modify the standards to increase your team's chances of winning.

2. Use 1" (2.5 cm) of *washed* sand or gravel.

3. Anchor your plants so they don't float.

4. Good plants to use are Elodea, Valisneria, Sagittaria and Cabomba. Ask your local fish store for other plants.

5. Dechlorinate the water with chemicals, or let it stand at least 24 hours before placing the fish in it.

6. Fill jars three-fourths full of water.

7. Use snails as scavengers to get rid of the fish's waste materials.

8. Place in indirect diffused light.

TLC10137 Copyright © Teaching & Learning Company, Carthage, IL 62321-0010

Name _____

Ecosystem Freedom

You are encouraged to try to keep your fish healthy longer by varying any factor in the ecosystem.

1. Vary the kind or amount of water.

2. Vary the kind or amount of plants.

3. Vary the kind or amount of snails.

4. Use sand, gravel, pebbles or "?"

5. Final feeding or special reserve food placed in the jar before sealing.

6. Special light treatment. Any special lights must be provided by you and will be turned off after school.

7. Type of chemical or vitamin treatment before sealing.

8. Describe your ecosystem freedom plans below. _____

_____

_____

_____

_____

Materials Needed: You will need wide-mouth gallon (liter) jars with screw-on lids. Try asking the cafeteria, a restaurant or your students. Buy healthy fish that are almost the same size. You will need snails plus some spare plants and gravel.

For the Teacher: Some parents and children may rightfully worry about the health of the fish. Emphasize that they will be checked constantly and moved to the class aquarium at the first sign of trouble.

TLC10137 Copyright © Teaching & Learning Company, Carthage, IL 62321-0010

Will Animals Disappear from the Earth?

Dinosaurs Are Only in the Movies

Dinosaurs roamed the world millions of years ago. Now they are all extinct.

Every plant and animal has a purpose. The bee gets its food from flowers. In return, bees help flowers to change into seeds and fruit. Wouldn't this world be in bad shape if bees became extinct?

There were once millions of passenger pigeons in America. They often traveled 100 miles (161 km) a day in huge flocks. Passenger pigeons are now extinct. They were hunted as food and sold for as little as two cents. The last known passenger pigeon died in 1914 in a Cincinnati zoo.

The California condor is the largest bird in North America. It can weigh 25 pounds (11 kg) and have a wingspread of 10 feet (3 m). Condors are in danger of becoming extinct. The food they eat is scarce. Hunters have shot them. They breed slowly. Only one egg is laid every other year. They are difficult to breed in captivity. The 50 plus remaining condors live in breeding centers or sheltered areas in a national forest near Los Angeles.

Endangered Species Cards

THEY ARE ALL EXTINCT

Passenger pigeon

Dodo

Great auk

You can learn about endangered species by doing some research. On the next page is a partial list of endangered species. Your class is going to study endangered species by making a class set of endangered species cards.

TLC10137 Copyright © Teaching & Learning Company, Carthage, IL 62321-0010

Name _____

1. All cards will be standard 8" x 5" (20 x 13 cm) file cards.

2. Your team can make two to four endangered species cards.

3. Each card should have a name and drawing or photo of the species on one side.

4. The other side should contain all the facts you can find about its environment, location, food requirements, etc.

5. You will be given class and outside time for research.

6. Make each endangered species card a thing of beauty.

PARTIAL LIST OF ENDANGERED SPECIES

Whale	West African Ostrich	California Sea Otter
Mountain Gorilla	Florida Manatee	Giant Anteater
Koala Bear	Trumpeter Swan	Giant Armadillo
Bald Eagle	Harp Seal	Snow Leopard
Grizzly Bear	White and Black Rhino	Desert Bighorn
Bighorn Sheep	Bengal Tiger	Orangutan
Loggerhead Turtle	Mountain Goat	Sea Otter

Endangered Species Debate

Sometimes animal protection conflicts with the needs of people. Suppose a much-needed dam is being built to save water, provide electricity and prevent flooding. The water filling up the dam will cover areas that contain an endangered species. In a recent real case, a Tennessee dam threatened to destroy a fish called the Snail Darter.

The Snail Darter deserves protection. People need the dam. Could you make a case for protecting the Snail Darters? Could you argue that the dam and people's needs are more important? It's time for an endangered species debate.

1. Your teacher will ask teams to debate both sides of the controversy.

2. Two teams should practice for a debate on the dam issue.

3. Other teams can choose to debate on protecting whales, the Canadian harp seals or "?"

4. The endangered species debates will take place on _____.

5. Don't be afraid to be on the unpopular side of the debate.

6. If your team prefers, you can challenge any other team to debate on **any** environmental issue. Don't confine yourself to endangered species.

7. Check the newspapers for local environmental issues to debate.

Materials Needed: You will need a quantity of 8" x 5" (20 x 13 cm) cards and a collection of endangered species literature.

TLC10137 Copyright © Teaching & Learning Company, Carthage, IL 62321-0010

NEWTON'S
ACTION LAB

Environment

14

Garbage Lab: Disposing of Man's Wastes

Garbage Galore

Because of higher standards of living and the population explosion, we are accumulating garbage at an alarming rate. The collection of food wastes, paper, glass, garden cuttings, metals, etc., is presenting a costly headache to all our cities. Finding the best means, place and financing for garbage disposal is one of America's unsolved problems.

The average American family produces about 100 pounds (45 kg) of garbage and trash each week. It costs over four billion dollars a year to collect and dispose of these wastes. Almost 50% of our trash is made of paper products. Glass and metal wastes add up to another 25%. Americans recycle only 10% of their trash. Japan recycles over 50%.

Garbage Brainstorming

A news article headline stated that "There's Profit in Trash." The article told of many ways that garbage can be used profitably. Canyons in Los Angeles are being filled with garbage and covered with soil to make new parks. One company has invented a process for making wastes into crude oil for gasoline. Dupage County, Illinois, piled their garbage into a mountain and converted it to a winter ski slope.

Name _____

Your team can earn extra points by listing your six **best** ideas for using garbage. **Only list your six best.** Be creative!

1. _____
2. _____
3. _____
4. _____
5. _____
6. _____

Milk Carton Madness

This investigation will deal mainly with the packaging material used in milk cartons. Your task will be to find valuable uses for milk cartons. Help save Americans from drowning in their own garbage. Develop uses of such merit that neighbors will be raiding each other's garbage cans for milk cartons.

Don't stand there! Start drinking more milk so you can accumulate cartons to use for your experiments. The small cartons from your school cafeteria work fine.

1. Your team's job is to develop new uses for milk cartons.

2. Your milk carton creations will be presented to the class on _____.

3. There are two categories explained below.

4. You must have at least one entry in each category.

5. You may have up to two entries in each category.

6. Judging will be on the basis of: **originality, workmanship** and **esthetic appearance**.

7. Include a *simple sketch* and *brief explanation* for the categories below.

Category 1:   A child or adult *game* developed from all or part of **milk cartons**.

   Example: A set of building blocks

Category 2:   Any novel use developed from **milk cartons**.

   Example: An insect cage

Materials Needed: You and your students should start saving paper milk cartons. Any size paper milk carton is acceptable.

For the Teacher: Turn your students loose. They can have a lot of fun and be creative as they recycle. Invite other classes in to see your recycled projects.

TLC10137 Copyright © Teaching & Learning Company, Carthage, IL 62321-0010

Name _____

Recycling Paper

Let's Use It Over and Over Again

Each year America buries trash that may contain valuable, salvageable material. Thrown out are iron, steel, copper, aluminum, glass, plastic and tons of paper. How to recycle these valuable materials is a problem awaiting a **technical** and **economical** solution. Technically, we must develop efficient recycling methods and devices. Economically, these recycling methods must make it cheaper to recycle than to produce a product from all new materials. Recycled paper sometimes costs more than paper made from newly cut trees. Recycled paper is often not as good a quality as the original paper it was made from.

Recycling paper has many secondary advantages. Suppose you made a ton of paper from 100% recycled waste paper. Here is what you would save.

- 17 trees
- 7000 gallons (264,600 l) of water
- 3 cubic yards of landfill
- 60 pounds (27 kg) of air polluting contaminants
- Over 100 dollars in electric energy

You Can Recycle Paper

1. You will find one-eighth sheet of newspaper and a baby food jar in your kit.

2. Tear the newspaper into the *smallest* pieces you can. Place the shredded pieces into the baby food jar. All team members should help in the tearing.

3. Add 30 milliliters of water to the jar with the paper.

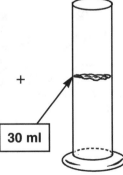

30 ml

TLC10137 Copyright © Teaching & Learning Company, Carthage, IL 62321-0010

Name _____

Cover tightly

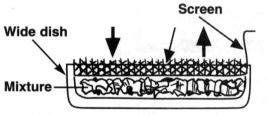

4. Rub the water-paper mixture with your fingers for **one** full minute. This will start the process of breaking the paper into its cellulose fibers.

5. Cover the jar tightly. Shake the jar **vigorously** for **two** full minutes. Again, let the team members rotate doing the shaking.

6. Remove the lid. Use a spoon to stir vigorously for another **two** minutes.

7. Add 15 more milliliters of water.

8. Cover and shake vigorously for **one** full minute.

9. Remove the lid. Add **one level** teaspoon (5 ml) of cornstarch. The cornstarch will act as a "binder" to glue the cellulose fibers together for your recycled paper.

10. Add 25 drops of chlorine bleach. This is to bleach out the newspaper ink and make your recycled paper lighter.

Caution! Bleach can stain your clothes.

11. Stir the mixture with a spoon for **two** full minutes.

Now you must use "technology" to do the final mixing.

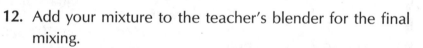

Wide dish **Screen**

Mixture

12. Add your mixture to the teacher's blender for the final mixing.

13. Your teacher will pour some of the blended mixture into a dish. Take it back to your lab area.

14. Lower your bent screen in and out of the mixture until a layer of fibers completely covers the screen. If your mixture is too thick, use your finger to place a thin layer of the mixture on your screen.

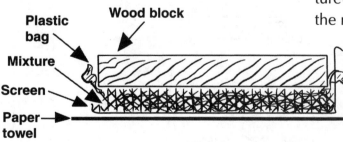

Plastic bag **Wood block**

Mixture

Screen

Paper towel

15. Set the wet screen on a paper towel with the paper mixture up.

16. Place a plastic bag on top of the paper mixture.

17. Use the block of wood to press gently on the plastic bag. The pressure of the wood block will squeeze the excess water out of your recycled paper.

44

Name _____

18. Press a little harder to get even more water out.

19. Use a new dry paper towel and repeat the squeezing.

20. Remove the block of wood, the plastic bag and the wet paper towel.

21. Give your paper-loaded screen to the teacher for overnight drying. Mark it in some way to identify your team.

Clean up your lab kit so another class may use it.

Comparing Your Recycled Paper with Notebook Paper

	Recycled Paper	Notebook Paper
Compare their colors.		
Compare their gloss (shine).		
Compare their texture (how they feel).		
Compare their ability to bend.		
Compare their ability to be torn.		
Use a ball-point pen to write on each. Compare their ability to take ink.		
Compare their ability to absorb a drop of water.		

On the basis of your results so far, name three best possible uses for your recycled

paper. _____

_____

TLC10137 Copyright © Teaching & Learning Company, Carthage, IL 62321-0010

Name _____

Creative Paper Test

So far your team has tried some simple tests to compare papers. Now it's time for your team to develop a more creative paper test. Here is a form for your paper test.

1. What characteristics of paper do you plan to test? _____

   _____

   _____

   _____

2. Sketch how your experiment will look.

3. What are your test results and conclusions? _____

   _____

   _____

   _____

Materials Needed: You will need covered baby food jars, paper towels, newspaper, 50-milliliter graduates, water, eyedroppers, dishes, plastic bags, teaspoons, cornstarch, wood blocks and small sections of wire screen. The wire screens should fit into the dish. Make them with a right angle bend to use as a handle.

For the Teacher: This is a complicated lab. It takes about 30 minutes one day and 30 minutes the next. You can substitute an egg beater for the blender. Combine two teams' mixtures if needed. You can mark off jars as graduates. The screen openings are vital. Try some beforehand. Tape the screen edges for safety.

The creative paper test is optional. You could skip it or have teams earn extra credit doing it at home.

TLC10137 Copyright © Teaching & Learning Company, Carthage, IL 62321-0010

What's Your Population I.Q.?

Instructions

1. You will take this I.Q. test by yourself without your team.

2. Answer true or false on the line to the left of each statement.

3. Make the best population guesses you can.

4. Your teacher will give you the correct answers after you have completed the entire test.

5. Place an *X* over any wrong answers.

6. Count the number of *X*s to determine your population I.Q. Use the ratings in the box.

0-3 Wrong–**Wizard**   4-7 Wrong–**Smart**

8-13 Wrong–**Normal**

14-20 Wrong–**You are surplus population**

Population I.Q. Test

Answer true or false.

_____ 1. There were less than a billion people on Earth back in the year 1800.

_____ 2. There are about 4 billion people on Earth now.

TLC10137 Copyright © Teaching & Learning Company, Carthage, IL 62321-0010

Name _____

_____ 3. California has more people than any other state.

_____ 4. China has over a billion people.

_____ 5. Senior citizens over 65 are the fastest growing part of the United States population.

_____ 6. There are more males than females in the United States.

_____ 7. A male baby born in the United States can expect to live longer than a female baby.

_____ 8. The present population of the United States is about 250 million.

_____ 9. The slowest population growth takes place in the poorest countries.

_____ 10. Immigration accounts for 25% of the United States' population growth.

_____ 11. A child born and raised in Sweden can expect to live longer than a child born and raised in the United States.

_____ 12. One of the world's slowest population growths is found in Japan.

_____ 13. The life expectancy of a child born at the same time as George Washington was 50 years.

_____ 14. Geriatrics is the study of older people and their problems.

_____ 15. The largest city in the entire world is New York City.

_____ 16. After China, the second most populated country in the world is India.

_____ 17. The country with the most people living in poverty is Egypt.

_____ 18. The population of Sweden actually goes down each year.

_____ 19. Japan has more people than Brazil.

_____ 20. The population of the United States is predicted to double in 100 years.

48

TLC10137 Copyright © Teaching & Learning Company, Carthage, IL 62321-0010

Population Explosion Problem

Too Many People

MOMMY —
WHAT'S FRESH AIR?

Our future on planet Earth is threatened by our population explosion. People consume more and more of the Earth's dwindling resources. People pollute, upset nature's balance and exterminate wildlife.

Back in 1900, there were only 1 1/2 billion people on Earth. Today, there are close to six billion people struggling to survive on Earth.

Columbus discovered America in 1492. There were an estimated five million Native Americans in what is now the United States. Today almost 250 million people live in the United States.

Americans make up only 5% of the world's large population. Yet we consume 25% of the world's oil and most other resources. We pollute the Earth by giving off 25% of the world's carbon dioxide.

How Fast Did We Grow?

A graph can present a picture of how the U.S. population has soared. Your team is to use the data table at the right to construct a graph on the following page of U.S. population growth.

1. An *X* has been drawn for the first data point.

2. Draw *X*s at the other data points. Your teacher will demonstrate this.

3. Use color to draw a smooth line through all data points.

4. Use color to extend a smooth **dotted** line to the year 2050.

5. What does your graph predict will be the U.S. population in the year 2050? _____ people

Year	Population in the U.S. (in millions)
1800	5
1850	23
1900	76
1950	150
1970	200
1980	225
1990	250

TLC10137 Copyright © Teaching & Learning Company, Carthage, IL 62321-0010

Name _____

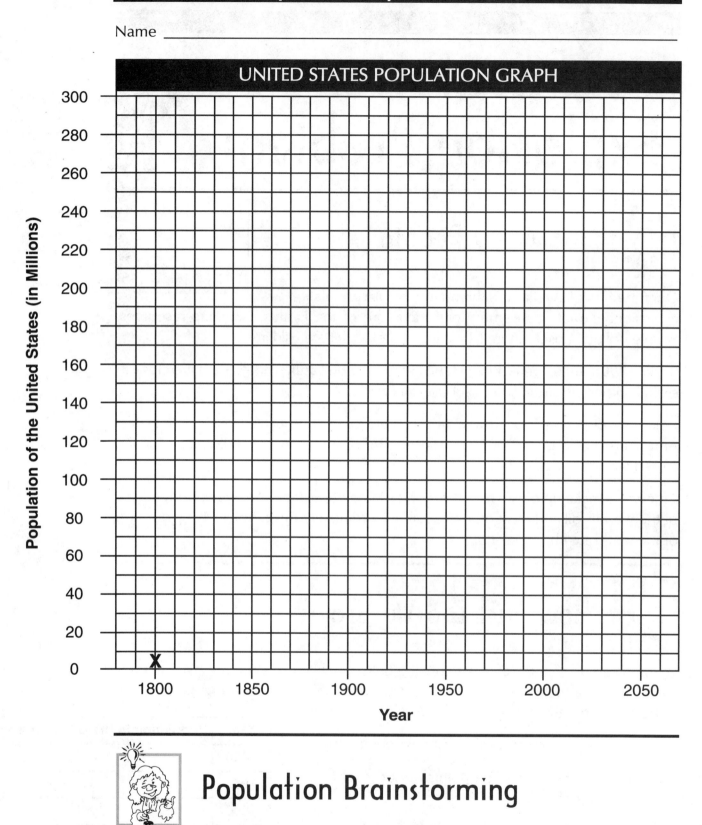

UNITED STATES POPULATION GRAPH

Population of the United States (in Millions)

300
280
260
240
220
200
180
160
140
120
100
80
60
40
20
0

X

1800   1850   1900   1950   2000   2050

Year

Population Brainstorming

Your team will be given 10 minutes to brainstorm one of the topics listed on the following page. Brainstorming involves freeing your mind to create real or possibly "way out" solutions. You may use ideas you have read or heard about, personal experiences or original thoughts that occur to you. The teacher will either assign your team one of the topics or allow you to choose the one that interests you.

50

Name _____

List your best suggestions on a sheet of paper to be read to the class by one member of your team. You will be given 10 minutes for brainstorming and three minutes for the oral report to the class. The team grade will be determined by how well your ideas are thought out and presented.

POPULATION TOPICS

1. Should immigration to the U.S. be completely restricted to save our resources for Americans?

2. What can be done to encourage people to move out of the cities and into the less crowded rural areas?

3. What should be the characteristics of a future super city that could handle large populations?

4. Should euthanasia (mercy killing) be made legal? Euthanasia involves putting people to death painlessly if they are extremely old or suffering from an incurable or painful disease.

5. How can America help poorer countries such as India and Latin American to cope with their population problems?

6. What legal and moral ways can be found to limit families to only two children?

7. Should abortion be made legal in the United States? Try to cover both sides of this moral and legal question.

8. What would be some effective ways (besides #6 and #7) to control population growth in the United States?

9. What can be done to provide the extra food, energy and other resources needed if the United States population continues to grow?

10. Should scientists be allowed to try to breed super-human people by selection of superior couples?

11. Any population topic of your choice. Obtain teacher approval for your subject.

Materials Needed: You may need some colored pens, pencils or markers.

For the Teacher: Your students may need some help with the graph. The predicted year 2050 population may be way off. Many factors are at work in the U.S. curbing population growth.

Name _____

Saving Solar Energy

Energy in Our Lives

Everyone knows what *energy* is, yet few can define it. People have energy, coal has energy, food has energy, ocean waves have energy and the sun has energy. The story of civilization is the story of man learning to use energy. The crowning achievement of science is the discovery of how to harness energy to meet our everyday needs.

Energy is all around us and within us. In fact, we live in an ocean of energy. As both you and a plant grow, you use energy. The flickering flame of a candle and the beam of light from a flashlight are displays of energy. The blowing wind and the warmth and light of the sun are energy. The gravitational pull of planets and the magnetic pull of magnets represent energy. In one form or another, energy is "locked" into every speck of dust in the universe.

Energy from the Sun

Let's suppose that we found a way to harness just 1% of the sun's energy that strikes the Earth. That would provide all the energy needs of the entire world.

Practically all our energy comes from the sun. Oil came from microscopic creatures that lived and died in the sunlit oceans.

1. Explain how coal is really trapped sunlight. _____

_____

2. Explain how wind energy is really caused by sunlight. **Hint:** Sunlight warms the Earth. The Earth warms the air. Explain the rest. _____

_____

_____

52

TLC10137 Copyright © Teaching & Learning Company, Carthage, IL 62321-0010

Name _____

3. Explain how the energy in our food really comes from sunlight. _____

_____

_____

More and more of our homes are being heated with solar energy. This activity will demonstrate how the sun's energy can be captured.

a. You will be given a black and a white can.

b. Fill both three-fourths full of water. Just guess at the three-fourths, but make sure both cans are filled to the **same** level.

c. Place them outside so that both cans get the same amount of solar energy.

d. Wait 20 to 30 minutes.

e. Measure the temperature in each can.

Black can _____ degrees   White can _____ degrees

Difference _____ degrees

f. Which color absorbed the most solar energy? _____

You Can Save Energy

The odds are that half the energy used in your home and car is wasted. This is equal to hundreds of dollars annually. Where is all this wasted energy? It may be wasted in your non-insulated home that leaks heat to the outdoors. It may be wasted in your constantly running television. It may be wasted in your new car that gets very few miles (kilometers) per gallon (liter). It may be wasted by you and your life-style. You, and only you, can conserve energy instead of wasting it.

Saving energy is as important as finding new sources of energy. How can you help save energy at home and at school?

1. Your team should come up with your four **best** energy-saving ideas in each category.

2. Saving energy in the kitchen. _____

_____

_____

Name _____

3. Saving energy in the bathroom. _____

_____

_____

_____

4. Saving energy in the laundry room. _____

_____

_____

_____

5. Saving energy in the rest of the house. _____

_____

_____

_____

6. Saving energy in your classroom. _____

_____

_____

_____

7. Saving energy in your school. _____

_____

_____

_____

Materials Needed: You will need thermometers and two painted cans per team.

For the Teacher: Your students may need help with the concept that most energy comes from the sun. Coal used to be plants that grew in the sun. Unequal heating of the Earth's surface causes winds. A light bulb gives off heat and light energy. That energy may come from water falling from a dam. The water behind the dam came from rain. It was the sun's energy that lifted the rain to the skies.

Use any two similar cans. Soda cans work but slightly bigger cans are better. Paint some cans shiny white. Paint the others dull black. Paint the tops where required.

Students can rotate and share thermometers. Use your finger to determine relative warmth if there are no thermometers available.

Use strong lights to replace the sun during bad weather.

TLC10137 Copyright © Teaching & Learning Company, Carthage, IL 62321-0010

NEWTON'S
ACTION LAB

Environment
19

Kilowatt Kaper: A Study of Energy

Computing Your Energy Costs

You know there is an energy shortage. There will continue to be an energy shortage in your lifetime. We waste too much energy. We waste too much oil, gas and coal.

In 1930 the average American home had 25 appliances. Your home today probably has over 100 appliances. All these appliances use, and sometimes waste, precious energy. This activity is designed to make you aware of how energy might be saved in **your** home.

If possible, bring in an electric bill from home. Otherwise, share a team member's bill.

	Example	Your Data
1. What is the total cost of your most recent *electric* bill? Use the amount for electricity only on your bill at home. Ask your parents for help. Don't include any charges for water or sewer service.	$231.50	
2. Find out from your bill how many kilowatt hours you consumed. Kilowatt hours are a measure of the amount of the energy you use. On the bill it is given as KWH. A 100-watt light bulb uses one KWH if burned for 10 hours.	4237 KWH	
3. Calculate the cost for each KWH. Do this by dividing the number 2 answer into the number 1 answer. See the example. Round off your answer to the nearest penny.	$\dfrac{\$231.50}{4237} = \$.05$	

Now you need to learn how to read an electric meter.

1. Read from left to right.

2. Note that some dials read clockwise and others read counterclockwise.

3. If a pointer is between two numbers, read the smallest number.

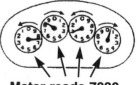

Meter reads 7025   **Meter reads 7830**

Name _____

Do the following readings on your home electric meter:

	Example	Your Data
4. Take a look at your electric meter. Observe the aluminum wheel which turns around as you use electricity. What is the reading in KWH for the first day?	31,623 KWH	
5. Take another reading one day later at about the same time as the first day. Record the KWH.	31,767 KWH	
6. Subtract your answer to number 4 from your answer to number 5. This will give you the number of KWH your family used in one day.	31,767 - 31,623 144 KWH	
7. Multiply the answer to number 6 by the cost for each KWH that you found in number 3. This will give you the cost of your family electricity for *one day*.	144 KWH x .05 $7.20	

Counting Your Home Kilowatts

Knowing which appliance is costing you the most may help you to decide where to start conserving. Pulling out your electric clock does not help as it only uses two KWH per month. Notice that an electric clothes dryer gulps energy. Save by only running it on a full load. The average home uses about 100 KWH per month for lighting. How much of this could be saved by simply turning off lights in empty rooms?

The chart on the next page shows the monthly KWH consumed by the **average** home appliance. Appliances differ widely, but these numbers are close enough to use.

1. Write the number of appliances of each kind that you have in your home in column A.

2. Multiply this number of appliances by the estimated KWH given for each appliance. Write your answer in column B.

TLC10137 Copyright © Teaching & Learning Company, Carthage, IL 62321-0010

Kilowatt Kaper: A Study of Energy

Name _____

HOME APPLIANCE DATA TABLE

Appliances	Estimated KWH Used per Month	A No. of Appliances	B Total KWH Used per Month
Central Air Conditioning (summer only) 5000 watts	700		
Blanket (electric) 180 watts	12		
Broiler 1500 watts	8		
Clock (electric) 2 watts	2		
Coffee Maker (automatic) 900 watts	9		
Clothes Dryer (all electric) 3400 watts	90		
Clothes Dryer–gas (electric motor) 500 watts	9		
Dishwasher 1200 watts	30		
Food Blender 400 watts	1		
Food Waste Disposal 450 watts	3		
Food Freezer 400 watts	125		
Frying Pan (automatic) 1200 watts	16		
Grill (sandwich) or Waffle Iron 1200 watts	3		
Hair Dryer 400 watts	1		
Iron (hand) 1000 watts	12		
Radio 80 watts	7		
Radio (phonograph) 110 watts	9		
Range (electric) 1200 watts	97		
Refrigerator-Freezer 500 watts	130		
Television (color) 200 watts	40		
Toaster 1200 watts	3		
Vacuum Cleaner 600 watts	4		
Washing Machine 500 watts	9		
Water Heater (electric) 4500 watts (Note: Most homes have gas heaters.)	400		
Light Bulb, Incandescent (estimated average–100 watts)	10		
Light Bulb, Fluorescent (estimated average–40 watts)	4		
Total KWH used per month in your home (Add all numbers in column B.)			

TLC10137 Copyright © Teaching & Learning Company, Carthage, IL 62321-0010

Name _____

Discuss with your family how you can save electricity in your home. List at least eight good ways you and your family can conserve energy and save money on your electric bill.

1. _____

_____

2. _____

_____

3. _____

_____

4. _____

_____

5. _____

_____

6. _____

_____

7. _____

_____

8. _____

_____

Materials Needed: A mock-up of an electric meter with movable hands would be useful.

For the Teacher: This is mainly an individual lab that assumes student-parent interaction at home. The net result is a very positive image for you and your class.

Obtain the custodian's help to obtain school costs for one day. Read the school electric meter on two successive days. The cost will astound your students.

TLC10137 Copyright © Teaching & Learning Company, Carthage, IL 62321-0010

Name ______________________________

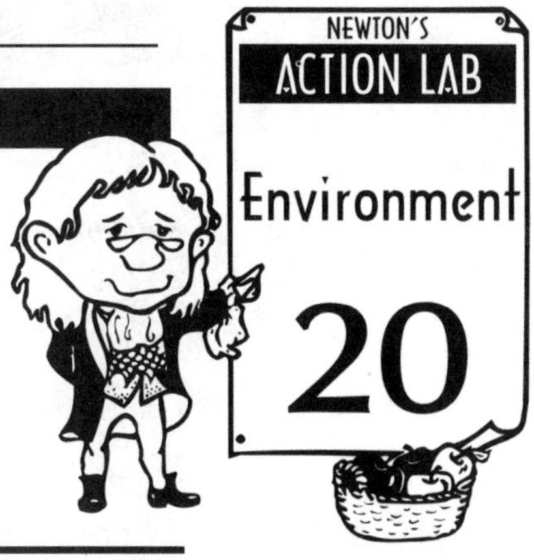

Environmental Symbols

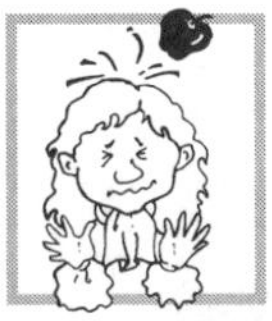

We Have Always Used Symbols

The use of symbols can be traced back as far as written history itself. People found quite early that symbols enable them to communicate quickly, easily and accurately. Here are some symbols used by Native Americans.

Sun	Star	Man	Rain	Sky	House	Fish

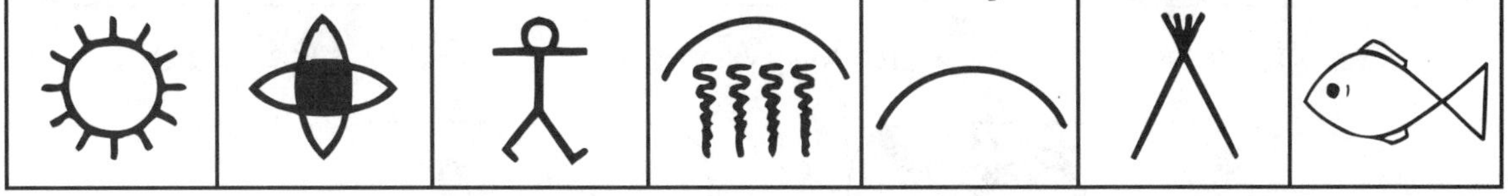

People in most fields of study use symbols to aid in communication. The advertising industry is an excellent example. Mathematicians use symbols such as = and %. These are well known, quickly recognized and save a great deal of space in equations.

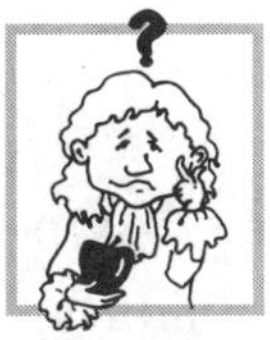

Do You Know Your Science Symbols?

Scientists invent and use many symbols. Look for clues to help you match the science symbols and their meanings. The symbols are in **random order**. Place the letter of the symbol you choose in the **Your Guess** column.

What It Is	Symbol	Your Guess
1. Math symbol for 3.14	A. ☼	
2. Electronic symbol for a battery	B. 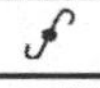	
3. Nuclear science symbol for an alpha particle	C. 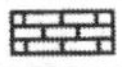	
4. Binary code for 13	D. 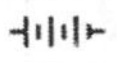	
5. Astronomy symbol for Mercury	E. α	
6. Geology symbol for limestone	F. Ag	
7. Biology symbol for spirillum bacteria	G. 1101	
8. Chemistry symbol for silver	H. 	
9. Warning symbol for radiation	I. π	
10. Weather symbol for hurricane	J. ☢	

TLC10137 Copyright © Teaching & Learning Company, Carthage, IL 62321-0010

Name _____

Creating Environmental Symbols

A good symbol is simple. A good symbol uses few or no words. Here are some common symbols recognized all over the world.

Telephone

Toilets, Women

Restaurant

No Smoking

Elevator

The field of environmental science is too new to have developed very many symbols. You will have a chance to design symbols for environmental pollution. Perhaps yours will become internationally accepted.

Do your work on scratch paper first. Then, when you like what you have designed, make a sketch of the symbol in the space provided. Be creative.

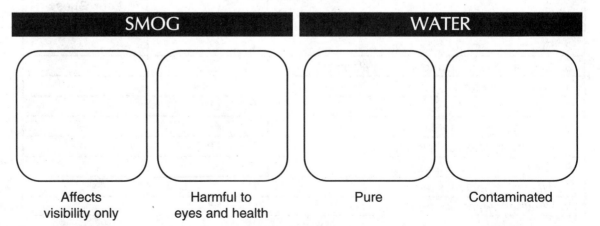

SMOG		WATER	
Affects visibility only	Harmful to eyes and health	Pure	Contaminated

TLC10137 Copyright © Teaching & Learning Company, Carthage, IL 62321-0010

Environmental Symbols

Name _____

FOOD

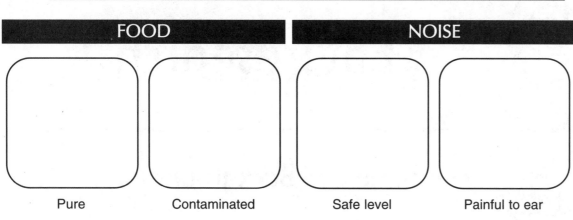

| Pure | Contaminated |

NOISE

| Safe level | Painful to ear |

RADIATION

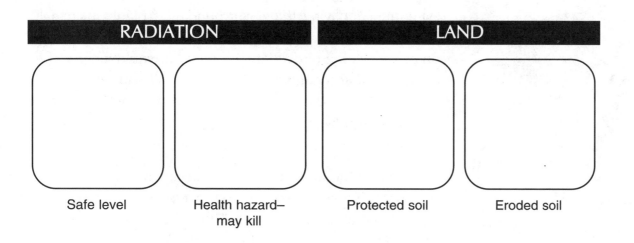

| Safe level | Health hazard– may kill |

LAND

| Protected soil | Eroded soil |

POPULATION

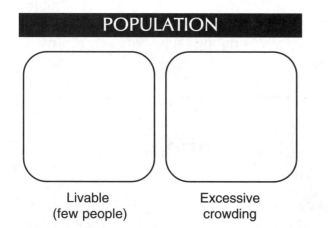

| Livable (few people) | Excessive crowding |

Materials Needed: You may need a supply of rulers, sharp pencils, pens, crayons or felt pens.

For the Teacher: Show, or have the students bring in, other kinds of symbols. Obtain copies of driving manuals that show traffic symbols. Encourage simplicity, humor and a minimum of words.

TLC10137 Copyright © Teaching & Learning Company, Carthage, IL 62321-0010

Name _____

Enviresearch

Environmental Background

The continuation of all forms of life on Earth depends on a proper **environment**. The *environment* is defined as all the living and nonliving things surrounding a plant or animal. For an insect, the environment includes the plants it feeds on as well as the birds that feed on it. It would include the temperature and humidity of the air as well as the chemical pesticides sprayed by man. Scientists who study the relationships between living things and their environment are called **ecologists**.

The greatest threat to life in the environment is people. The search for food and resources to provide for expanding populations has abused the Earth. Throughout history we have suffered from this abuse "of the Earth."

Environmental abuse can cause disasters. Some cities have health-threatening smog. Some harbors are filthy. Tankers spill oil. Endangered species are hunted. Garbage piles up. Treeless areas have mud slides during rains. The environment can be damaged in many ways by people.

Researching the Environment

Your team is about to begin a research project. You will be given about three weeks to research an environmental subject and report back to the class. Your report should be partly written, partly oral and partly visual aids such as charts and pictures.

Choose a subject of your choice. Following are some suggestions, but there are many more. Plan an interesting class report that will keep your classmates awake.

1. World population growth

2. Use of chemical and biological weapons in wars

62

Name _____

3. Nuclear energy as used for peaceful or military purposes

4. Storing nuclear wastes

5. Environmental pollution of the air or water

6. Global food shortage

7. Preservation or destruction of wilderness areas and wildlife

8. Ecological effects of chemicals including pesticides, lead and mercury

9. Environmental blight caused by noise, advertising signs and poorly planned cities and highways

10. Garbage disposal problems

11. Oil pollution by tankers or pipelines

12. Forest conservation

13. Acid rain

14. Global warming

15. Depletion of the ozone layer

16. Destruction of rain forests

17. Protecting endangered species

18. Soil conservation

19. Preserving natural resources for future generations

20. Asbestos danger

21. Factory pollution of lakes and rivers

22. Future energy sources

For the Teacher: Your main job is as advisor. Perhaps plan one period in the library for research. Collect the names, phone numbers and addresses of various environmental action groups. Encourage teams to have brief and interesting class reports. Good visual aids are important.

TLC10137 Copyright © Teaching & Learning Company, Carthage, IL 62321-0010

Answer Key

Symbiosis Data Table, page 23

1. Cow gives food, man feeds and protects cow.
2. parasitism
3. bacteria in nodules
4. oxygen-carbon dioxide exchange
5. mutualism
6. plants pollinated, bee gets nectar
7. parasitism
8. mutualism
9. commensalism mainly; a small amount of parasitism
10. whale
11. mutualism
12. parasitism
13. mutualism

We Need Trees, pages 28-29

1. oxygen
2. shade
3. lumber
4. furniture
5. boats
6. lemons
7. rubber
8. nuts
9. fuel
10. syrup

How Old Is Your Tree? page 30

Bonus: The General Sherman tree is about 3400 years old.

Population I.Q. Test, pages 47-48

1. True
2. False: Closer to $5\frac{1}{2}$ billion
3. True: Well over 20 million
4. True: Actually 1.1 billion
5. True: Senior citizens represent 12% of the population and that percent is increasing as the life span increases.
6. False: Females make up 51.4% of the total.
7. False: Females live up to seven years longer. Ask your students their opinion as to why women live longer.
8. True
9. False: Third World countries in Africa and Latin America have rapid population growth. Some families there have six to eight children.
10. True
11. True: Almost two years more
12. True: Birth control is popular.
13. False: Actually less than 35 years
14. True
15. False: New York City has about 18 million. Mexico City has 19.4 million. Mexico City may have 31 million people by the year 2000.
16. True: About 850 million people
17. False: The poorest country is Ethiopia with 80% of their people living in poverty.
18. True: There are more deaths than births in Sweden. This is also true of Denmark and Ireland.
19. False: Brazil has 150 million. Japan has only 122 million.
20. True: The doubling rate in Syria and Kenya is 20. This means that every 20 years their population increases two times.

Do You Know Your Science Symbols? page 59

1. I
2. D
3. E
4. G
5. A
6. C
7. H
8. F
9. J
10. B

64